ALISON HOLST'S
SOUP
BOOK

First published 1997 by
Hyndman Publishing
PO Box 5017, Dunedin
ISBN 1-877168-04-1

© TEXT: Alison Holst

DESIGNER: Rob Di Leva

PRODUCTION: De Leva Design

ILLUSTRATIONS: Clare Ferguson

PHOTOGRAPHER: Sal Criscillo

HOME ECONOMISTS: Alison Holst,
Dee Harris, Jane Ritchie,

PRINTING: Tablet Colour Print

2nd Reprint July 1997

COVER PHOTOGRAPH: Creamy Lentil
and Vegetable Soup (Page 45)

About this book

I LOVE soup, and get as much satisfaction out of making it as I do from eating it! My husband and children will tell you that, when the soup-making urge comes upon me, I will hover over my soup pot with great pleasure, and serve my masterpiece triumphantly, expecting my family to be delighted, even though it may be the hottest day of the year!

I associate soup with coming home as a child to the comfort of a loving mother, a warm kitchen, and a bowl of steaming soup ladled out of the bubbling pot on the stove.

This book contains all my favourite soup recipes, some old, and others new. Most require very little effort, and many are very quickly made, although some need to simmer quietly (but usually without attention) for several hours. In general, my soups cost very little, sometimes utilising bits and pieces which would otherwise be discarded, and often making the most of seasonal produce.

It's nice to know that soups are good healthy foods, containing fibre, vitamin and mineral-rich grains, vegetables and pulses in an easy-to-eat form. What's more, children who may turn up their noses at a recognisable vegetable, will often eat it quite willingly in soup.

Those of you who are keeping a watchful eye on the scales will be as delighted as I was to learn that people who eat soup regularly weigh less than people who don't. What a pleasing statistic!

I hope that you will make many of these recipes, with as much enjoyment as I do!

Good Cooking.

Alison Holst

Before you start!

When you are making soup, you do not need to measure ingredients nearly as accurately as you do when, for example, you are baking. A larger potato or smaller onion than intended will not spoil the soup you are making! Take care with seasonings, however, or your soups may be too salty, or too highly seasoned.

Use standard, metric (250ml) cups, and level, metric measuring (5ml) teaspoons and (15ml) tablespoons.

2 tablespoons of butter weigh 25 grams.

I used a 750 watt microwave oven. Cook foods a little more or less if yours is not the same.

A food processor or blender makes it easy and quick to puree foods, but a mouli (second hand or new) or a sieve will give you good results too.

For speed and convenience, I often use jars of minced garlic, chili and ginger, sliced lemon grass and green curry paste. These keep well in the refrigerator.

Some recipes call for ingredients such as fish sauce, sesame oil, coriander leaves, and fresh egg noodles. If you are not familiar with these, look in large supermarkets or stores stocking Asian ingredients.

Buy pesto and salsa, or make your own using the recipes at the back of the book.

Take care when heating low-fat milks. They catch on the bottom if not stirred often during cooking.

Contents

Oriental Coconut Soup

Eastern soups are excitingly different! Although this one takes only 20 minutes from start to finish, it provides an interesting mixture of hot and sour flavours. Choose from chicken, fish or vegetarian options.

For 2 large main or 4 starter servings:

400ml can coconut cream

2 cups chicken, fish or vegetable stock*

1 cup water

1 tsp minced or grated fresh ginger

2 Tbsp fish sauce

2–3 tsp curry powder

1 lime, finely grated rind and juice

½ tsp minced chili or 1 small fresh chili,
*   finely chopped*

1 Tbsp very finely sliced lemon grass

125–150g egg noodles

4 tsp sesame oil

200g chicken breast, fish fillets, or prawns

6 button mushrooms, thinly sliced

1 cup bean sprouts, optional

Measure the first 8 ingredients (down to and including minced chili) into a medium-sized pot. Add the lemon grass. (If using fresh lemon grass grate or finely chop the base of the stem only.) Stir to mix, and bring to the boil. Turn the heat down and simmer gently for 20 minutes.

Use yellowy, fresh egg noodles from Asian food stores or instant dried noodles (without flavour sachets) from your supermarket. Cook dried noodles according to the instructions on the packet, or cook fresh noodles briefly in salted boiling water. Drain and stir in 2 teaspoons of the sesame oil. Toss to mix and put aside.

Finely slice the chicken or fish. Mix these or the prawns with the remaining sesame oil and put aside too.

Just before serving, add the mushrooms, bean sprouts, noodles, chicken, fish or prawns to the hot stock, bring back to the boil and simmer for a few minutes, until the additions are cooked.

For interest let your family or friends spoon one or more of the following prepared ingredients into their bowls: chopped coriander leaves, Vietnamese mint, spring onions, hardboiled eggs, or roasted peanuts, freshly grated coconut, or lime wedges.

VARIATION: For a completely vegetarian version of this soup, use vegetarian stock* and replace the chicken or fish with bean curd or tofu.

HINT: You can now buy, in many supermarkets, minced ginger, minced garlic, minced chili and finely chopped lemon grass in jars which keep well in the refrigerator.

* Use homemade stock (page 55–58) or 2 teaspoons of instant stock powder in 2 cups of water.

Sour, Sweet & Hot Soup

Here is another interesting Asian soup, easy to make despite its long list of flavourings. Soured with lemon juice, sweetened with a little sugar, and heated with chili, it is deliciously different, well worth making with good stock.

For 4–6 servings:

6 cups chicken stock*

1 lemon or lime

2 Tbsp fish sauce

2 Tbsp sugar

2 Tbsp very finely sliced lemon grass**

1 tsp finely chopped garlic**

2 tsp minced or grated fresh ginger**

2 tsp ground coriander

½ tsp minced chili**

salt and pepper to taste

500g chicken breast, fish fillets, or prawns, optional

8–10 button mushrooms, optional

1 carrot, optional

2 small zucchini, optional

4 spring onions

2–3 Tbsp chopped fresh coriander

Measure the stock into a large pot. (For good results, use at least a litre of homemade chicken stock.)

Cut the lime or lemon into quarters and add these to the stock with the next seven ingredients. Bring to the boil, turn the heat down and simmer gently for 15 minutes.

Remove the lime or lemon quarters, squeezing the remaining juice from them into the soup. Taste carefully, adding salt, pepper and more lime or lemon juice if you like.

The soup tastes good like this, without any more solids, but the optional ingredients add extra flavour and substance to it. If you are using them, slice the boneless, skinless chicken or fish and the mushrooms thinly, and cut the carrot and zucchini into long, thin matchsticks. Stir whatever you are using into the soup, bring it back to the boil,

and simmer until additions are cooked.

Before serving, stir in the finely chopped spring onions and coriander leaves.

VARIATION: For vegetarian soup use homemade vegetable stock and add strips or cubes of firm tofu with the suggested vegetables.

* Use homemade stock (page 55–58) or 1 litre of homemade stock and no more than 2 teaspoons of instant stock powder in 2 cups of water.

** Use fresh, or from the jars described at the end of the recipe on page 4.

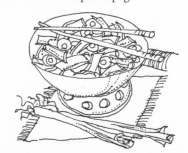

Wonton Soup

This soup was very popular with my children when they were at primary school. For a real treat, we would buy the wontons at a specialty Asian food store after school, then make the soup together!

For 4 large main or 8 starter servings:

4 cups cold chicken stock*

2 cups prepared vegetables, eg mushrooms, bean sprouts, spring onions, small spinach leaves, snow peas

4 cups water

1 Tbsp soya sauce

1 Tbsp sherry

½ tsp salt

32 wonton wrappers

Wonton Filling:

250g pork or beef mince

1 Tbsp oil

1 Tbsp sherry

1 Tbsp soya sauce

1 tsp cornflour

1 tsp sesame oil

¼ tsp salt

4 spring onions, chopped

Put the chicken stock and thinly sliced vegetables in a large pot and put aside.

In a large frypan, heat the water, soya sauce, sherry and salt until simmering.

Buy fresh or frozen wonton wrappers from an Asian food store or supermarket. If you buy them fresh, freeze the remainder.

To make the filling, mix all the filling ingredients, then divide into 32 small, portions, as evenly as possible. (Cut mixture into 4, then 8, then 16 then 32.)

Place a portion of filling in the centre of a wrapper then fold in half diagonally to form a triangle. Dampen one folded corner with water. Hold folded corners between thumbs and forefingers. With one middle finger, press filled area gently so the dampened corner can be brought towards, then under, the other folded corner. Pinch together firmly.

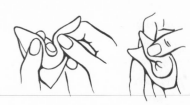

After you have made 4–6 wontons, drop them gently into the boiling liquid in the frypan, jiggling the pan so they do not stick to each other or the pan.

Cook for 5 minutes after liquid returns to the boil. Lift each, with a slotted spoon, into cold chicken stock when cooked. Prepare and cook the rest of the wontons, then pour the remaining liquid from the frypan into the pot.

To serve, heat carefully until the wontons have just heated through, then ladle into bowls. Sprinkle with chopped coriander leaves if desired.

* Use homemade chicken stock for this recipe (page 56–57).

"Dieters' Delight" Soup

This delicious, low calorie, highly flavoured soup is a real boon for dieters. Refrigerate, heating a bowlful for lunch, and to eat before your main meal. Despite the long ingredient list it takes less than half an hour to make.

For 12 cups, 6–8 large servings:

1–2 large onions
2 tsp olive or other oil
1 tsp dried oreganum
2 tsp ground cumin
¼ tsp dried thyme
2 tsp finely chopped garlic*
1 tsp minced or grated fresh ginger*
1–1½ tsp Thai green curry paste
4–6 large stalks celery
1–2 green or red peppers
500g cabbage
6 cups hot water plus 1 cup cold water
1 packet Cream of Chicken Soup
1 Tbsp cornflour
2 (400g) cans Italian or Mexican Tomatoes
2–3 Tbsp tomato paste
chopped fresh herbs
1 Tbsp pesto**

Cook the chopped onion in the oil in a large pot, over moderate heat for 5 minutes. Stir in the next 6 seasonings, and cook with the onion while you chop up, then add as each is prepared, the celery, peppers and cabbage. (Chop the cabbage into small chunky pieces rather than long shreds.) Add the hot water, bring to the boil and simmer for 5 minutes.

Mix the powdered soup, cornflour and cold water together to a smooth paste, then stir into the boiling vegetable mixture. When the soup has thickened, add the contents of the cans of tomatoes, the tomato paste, herbs and the pesto if you have it.

As soon as the soup boils again, remove from the heat. Taste and adjust the seasonings if necessary, until the soup has a really good flavour.

Refrigerate in covered containers as soon as the soup is cool enough. Heat up only as much as you need for each meal. Refrigerate for up to a week, or freeze for longer storage.

HINTS: I know that the ingredient list is long, but half are flavourings, without which the soup is boring!

Remember that the green curry paste contains chili, so, the more you add, the hotter you make the soup.

* Somewhat to my surprise, I found that the ready-prepared chopped or pureed garlic and ginger in jars gave the soup a stronger, better flavour than the fresh product. I suggest you use them.

** Use bought or homemade pesto (page 61).

Artichoke Soup

Jerusalem artichoke plants look very like sunflower plants, and are very easy to grow. The tubers under the plants look like knobbly potatoes, have a definite, mild and interesting flavour, and make the most wonderful soup.

For 4 servings:

500–600g Jerusalem artichokes
1 Tbsp butter
1–2 cloves garlic
1½ cups chicken stock (page 56) or 2 tsp
    instant stock powder in 1½ cups water
1 tsp sugar
½ tsp salt
1–1½ cups milk
about ¼ cup cream

Jerusalem artichokes are hard to peel because of their knobbly surface. For this soup they need not be peeled, but should be well scrubbed with a small brush, then cut into slices or chunks no more than 1cm thick.

Melt the butter in a medium-sized pot, add the finely chopped garlic and cook gently for about a minute, without browning. Add the sliced artichokes, stock or water and instant stock powder, sugar and salt.

Cover the pot and simmer for 10 minutes, or until the artichokes are tender when pierced with a knife.

Lift the pieces of artichoke from the pot with a slotted spoon and puree in a food processor, blender, or mouli, adding the cooking liquid gradually, after the vegetables are pulverised. Add the smaller amount of milk to the puree, process

again, then pour through a sieve, to remove any pieces of skin.

Stir in the cream, and add enough of the remaining milk to the soup until it reaches the consistency you like. (If you want a rich soup for a special occasion, add a little extra cream.)

Just before serving reheat the soup, adjusting the seasonings to bring out the full flavour of the artichokes.

Garnish each serving with a small amount of whipped or plain cream and some finely chopped parsley or chives.

HINT: If the greyish colour of this soup bothers you, cook a little spinach or pumpkin with the artichokes, so your soup looks more attractive.

WARNING: Jerusalem artichokes may upset some people's stomachs, causing wind! Do not give guests large servings of soup without telling them what they are eating!

Spiced Kumara Soup

The easiest vegetable soups are made from vegetables such as kumara, parsnips, Jerusalem artichokes and pumpkins, which need only to be cooked, pureed, then thinned down with stock or milk to make smooth, tasty, satisfying soups.

For 4–6 servings:

2 cloves garlic

½–1 tsp curry powder

75g butter

600g kumara

1½ cups water

2 tsp instant chicken stock powder or 1 tsp salt

about 3 cups milk

¼ cup cream, optional

Add the finely chopped garlic and curry powder to the butter in a large pot.

Peel the kumara thinly (a potato peeler does a good job) and cut them in half lengthways. Slice 1cm thick, crossways.

Cook the vegetables gently in the butter without browning, for 1–2 minutes, then add the water. Cover and cook for 10 minutes or until the kumara is tender.

Stir in the instant chicken stock or salt, then puree the vegetables and cooking liquid, thinning the puree with milk until the soup is the thickness you like.

Add cream for a richer soup, and reheat without boiling.

Spiced Parsnip Soup

Replace the kumara with the same weight of prepared parsnips, making the soup in exactly the same way.

Roasted Kumara or Parsnip Soup

Prepare a slightly larger quantity of either vegetable, cut them in larger chunks (about 2cm cubes), brush with oil and roast in a moderate oven with 2 quartered onions until the vegetables are tender and lightly browned. Cut off any dark brown pieces before pureeing, etc., as above. Because the colour of both soups is darker, you might like to roast some pumpkin pieces with the other vegetables, so the finished soup has an orange tinge.

...wonderful soup......

Pumpkin Soups

Pumpkins, available for most of the year, are so cheap at times, that they are almost given away! Pumpkin soup is so easy to make, cheerfully bright, and popular, that it is well worth making regularly in cold weather.

Quick Pumpkin Soup

Extra-easy and really low fat!

For 6–8 servings:

1kg prepared pumpkin
3 cups water
2 tsp instant chicken stock powder
2 tsp instant green herb stock powder
2 tsp sugar
½ tsp grated nutmeg
2 medium onions
2 cloves garlic
1–2 cups milk*

* Use skim milk for a very low fat soup.

Cut the pumpkin into 6–8 pieces. Remove the seeds, but not the skin, especially if it is thick. Weigh it at this stage.

Place in a large pot with the water, seasonings, quartered onions and peeled garlic. Cover and cook briskly for about 10 minutes, or until the pumpkin is soft, but still brightly coloured.

Remove the skin and puree everything else in a food processor, blender or mouli in several batches if necessary, or push through a sieve. Thin the puree, with milk, to the thickness you like.

Reheat and serve as is, or with a spoon of pesto (page 61) swirled on top, with croutons, Melba toast, crostini, garlic bread (pages 59–60), mousetraps, toasted cheese sandwiches or crusty bread.

Kumara, Pumpkin & Peanut Soup

This combination makes a popular and interesting soup with a complex flavour. It is good for a vegetarian main course.

For 4–6 servings:

1 large onion
1 tsp finely chopped garlic
2 Tbsp butter or oil
½ tsp curry powder
½ tsp freshly ground coriander seed
⅛–¼ tsp chili powder
1 fairly large (250g) kumara
250g pumpkin
4 cups chicken or vegetable stock (pages 55–57) or 2 tsp instant chicken stock powder in 4 cups water
½ tsp salt
2 Tbsp peanut butter

Pumpkin Soups

When you are using a large pumpkin to make any pumpkin soup, cook twice or three times as much as you need, and freeze what you do not need immediately in concentrated form, at the stage before you dilute the thick puree.

Cook the chopped onion and garlic over low heat in the butter or oil, in a medium-sized pot, until the onion is transparent. Add the curry powder, freshly ground coriander seeds, and chili powder (as much as you like for hotness) to the onion mixture and stir over moderate heat for about a minute.

Chop the prepared kumara and pumpkin into 1cm cubes. (Do not use more kumara or the soup will be too sweet.) Add the vegetables to the pot with the stock or instant stock powder and water, bring to the boil and simmer for about 15 minutes or until the vegetables are tender. Add salt then the peanut butter. (Too much overpowers the vegetables.)

Puree in a food processor, blender or mouli (or use a potato masher). Adjust seasonings and reheat. Serve topped with a swirl of yoghurt, coconut cream or with a few finely chopped roasted peanuts.

Spiced Pumpkin Soup

Added spices and coconut cream turn pumpkin soup into something quite exotic.

For 3–4 servings:

1 tsp finely chopped garlic
1 Tbsp oil
2 tsp ground cumin
1 tsp freshly ground coriander seeds
750g pumpkin
1 cup water
about 1 cup coconut cream
½ tsp salt
1 tsp Tabasco sauce

In a medium-sized pot, gently cook the garlic in the oil for about a minute, then add the ground cumin and the crushed coriander seeds and heat for another minute or two, until the spices are aromatic but have not darkened too much.

Add the pumpkin, cut in 1–2cm cubes, then cover and cook gently in the water for 10 minutes or until tender.

Puree the pumpkin, spices and cooking liquid in a food processor, blender or mouli, then add coconut cream, salt and Tabasco sauce in quantities to suit your taste.

Reheat when required and serve with crunchy bread and salad as the main course of a light meal, or at the start of a spicy Asian meal.

HINT: If you have green curry paste in your refrigerator, add ½–1 teaspoon to the oil just after you add the spices.

Curried Pumpkin & Bacon Soup

This soup is particularly tasty when made with smoky bacon. For variety, mash the vegetables to get a rough "country" texture at times, and on occasions, make quite a different soup by pureeing everything and adding a little cream.

For 4 servings:

500g pumpkin

3 bacon rashers

25g butter

2 onions

2 cloves garlic

½–1 tsp curry powder

3 (about 300g) potatoes

1 tsp salt

about 1 tsp sugar

2 cups water

extra water, milk, or cream

Scoop the seeds and pith out of the pumpkin, peel and cut into 5cm cubes. Weigh the pumpkin after preparing it.

Cut the rinds off the bacon, then chop the bacon into small pieces.

Brown the bacon rind and the pieces in a large pot, over moderate heat, adding a little of the butter if necessary. Lift out half of the cooked bacon pieces to use as a garnish and add the remaining butter, chopped onions, finely chopped garlic and curry powder (using the larger amount of curry powder for a definite curry flavour).

Cook over fairly low heat for about 5 minutes, until the onion is lightly browned and transparent.

Add the cubed pumpkin and the potatoes which have been peeled and cut in 2cm cubes, the salt, about half a teaspoon of sugar and the water.

Cover and simmer until the pumpkin and potato are tender, then remove and discard the bacon rinds.

To make a soup with a rough texture, mash the mixture with a potato masher.

For a smooth soup, puree, using a food processor, blender or mouli, pouring the mixture back into the pot through a sieve if you want a very smooth texture.

Thin with water, milk or cream (or a mixture of these) until the soup is the thickness you like. Taste and adjust the seasoning carefully, with more salt, pepper and the remaining sugar.

Reheat, without boiling, just before serving. Garnish each serving with some of the reserved bacon pieces, and with croutons (page 59).

Pumpkin Soup

Gardeners' Tomato Soup

Gardeners' Tomato Soup

This soup calls for really red, ripe, flavourful tomatoes. If your tomatoes are not at their best, you are better to use canned tomatoes. We like this soup when it is chunky, but you can puree it if you want to.

For 4 large servings:

1 large onion
25g butter
1 tsp finely chopped garlic
1 Tbsp flour
1 tsp sugar
1 tsp instant green herb stock powder or
    $\frac{1}{2}$ tsp salt
$\frac{1}{2}$ tsp paprika
1 cup water
750g ripe red tomatoes
basil, thyme and oreganum
$\frac{1}{2}$ tsp ground cumin, optional
Tabasco sauce, optional
freshly ground black pepper
$\frac{1}{4}$ cup chopped parsley

For more tomato soups see pages 48, 49.

Chop the onion finely and cook in the butter without browning for 5 minutes or until tender. Do not hurry this step.

Stir in the finely chopped garlic and cook for a minute longer, then mix in the flour and cook a little longer.

Add the next four ingredients and simmer for another 5 minutes, while you halve the tomatoes, shake out most of their seeds and cut each half into 9 or 16 cubes, depending on their size.

Add the tomatoes and cook gently for 5–10 minutes longer.

While it is simmering, flavour the soup with fresh or dried herbs, using amounts to suit your taste. (If you are not sure what quantities to use, try about $\frac{1}{2}$ teaspoon of dried oreganum or $\frac{1}{4}$ teaspoon of dried thyme, or a tablespoon of chopped fresh basil.)

If you do not add any herbs, add the cumin, which, although not essential, adds good flavour. Add Tabasco sauce if you like.

Add pepper to taste, stir in the chopped parsley, adjust saltiness and sweetness to get a nice balance, and serve.

Serve with croutons, crostini, or garlic bread (pages 59–60).

VARIATIONS: For a smooth soup, puree and sieve before adding the parsley.

Cream of Tomato Soup

Stir in $\frac{1}{4}$ – $\frac{1}{2}$ cup of cream just before serving.

Spinach Soup

As long as you do not overcook it, this soup is a wonderful bright green. A little added cream "softens" the flavour and makes this soup popular with many people who do not enjoy plainly cooked spinach.

For 6–8 servings:
1 large onion or the white part of 2 leeks
1 Tbsp butter
½ tsp freshly grated nutmeg
2 large potatoes
3 cups chicken or vegetable stock (pages 55–57) or 2 tsp instant stock powder in 3 cups water
250g spinach
½ cup cream
½ cup milk
salt and pepper

Finely chop or slice the onion or leeks and add to the melted butter in a fairly large pot. Add the freshly grated nutmeg and cook over low to moderate heat for 5–10 minutes, without browning.

Scrub the potatoes and cut into 1cm cubes. Add to the pot with the stock or instant stock powder and water.

Cover and bring to the boil, simmering for about 15 minutes, or until the potatoes are tender. Add the well-washed, chopped spinach and simmer for 3–4 minutes longer, until the spinach is tender but is still bright green.

Puree the vegetables and liquid in a food processor, blender or mouli, in several batches if necessary.

Strain the pureed soup back into the pot, through a sieve. Whisk in the cream and milk. Thin further if desired with extra milk or cream or with stock.

Taste, and adjust the seasoning if necessary, adding extra salt, freshly ground pepper and nutmeg.

Reheat briefly just before serving plain, with a swirl of plain or lightly whipped cream, or with croutons, Melba toast or cheesy pastry croutons (pages 59–60).

VARIATION: If preferred, make this soup with young silver beet leaves instead of spinach. Trim away the light coloured central ribs on the leaves, before chopping and cooking it. The flavour is good but slightly different, and the colour is not as bright.

Asparagus Soup

Eat this soup as soon as it is made, or freeze it, if you are lucky enough to have access to a lot of cheap, fresh asparagus. This soup freezes extremely well — much better, I think, than plain asparagus.

For 6–8 servings:

2 cloves garlic
50g butter
1/4 cup flour
500g tender asparagus
2 cups water
1 1/4 cups cream
1/2 tsp salt
freshly ground black pepper

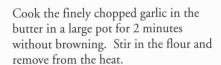

Cook the finely chopped garlic in the butter in a large pot for 2 minutes without browning. Stir in the flour and remove from the heat.

Before weighing the asparagus, snap off and discard the tough, lower ends of the stalks. Grate the asparagus, using the appropriate blade of a food processor or a hand held grater. (Hold the bunch of asparagus at right angles to the grater.)

In another pot, bring the water to the boil, add the asparagus and boil for 2 minutes, until bright green and barely tender.

Drain the cooking liquid into the butter and flour mixture and bring to the boil, stirring all the time. Add the cooked asparagus and the cream, and bring back to the boil.

If serving immediately, thin to desired consistency with milk, vegetable stock, or water. Season to taste with salt and pepper if necessary.

If freezing do not thin, but cool the thick, undiluted soup as quickly as possible, by standing the pot in a large container of cold or iced water, so the asparagus keeps its bright colour.

When serving the soup from your freezer, bring the thawed soup to the boil, thin as required, then adjust seasonings.

Hand around crostini or garlic bread (pages 59–60).

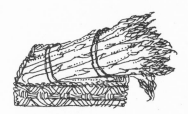

Mushroom Soup

Over the years I have often exclaimed that nothing tastes as good as the soup I make from field mushrooms. Now I find, however, that the large flat, brown-gilled mushrooms from the supermarkets make wonderful soup. Try for yourself!

For 6 servings:

2 medium onions

3 Tbsp butter

2 cloves garlic

4 medium (150g) flat brown mushrooms

¼ tsp dried thyme

3 Tbsp flour

*2 cups chicken stock (page 56) or 2 tsp
    instant stock powder in 2 cups water*

½ tsp salt

pepper to taste

1 Tbsp sherry, optional

1 Tbsp balsamic or wine vinegar

2 cups milk

Cook the chopped onions in the butter in a large pot, over a medium heat for about 5 minutes until they are lightly browned. Add the finely chopped garlic and cook for 1–2 minutes longer.

Chop the mushrooms finely and add to the onions with the thyme. Cook for another 5 minutes, stirring frequently.

Stir in the flour, and cook until it has lightly browned too, then add the stock, or water and instant stock powder, the salt and pepper, sherry and balsamic or wine vinegar. Stir well to mix and bring to the boil, then turn down and simmer gently for 5–10 minutes.

Whisk or stir in the milk, heat until almost boiling, then serve.

VARIATION: I think that it is nice to have some chunky pieces through Brown Mushroom Soup, but if you prefer a smooth, creamier soup, proceed as far as boiling the soup before the milk is added. Pour it through a sieve, catching all the chunky pieces in it. Put these in a food processor, blender or mouli with a little of the strained liquid, and process to a thick puree. Mix this, the strained mixture and the milk, then reheat almost to boiling, OR strain this mixture through a coarse sieve, pressing out all the liquid from the solids, if you want an even smoother soup.

Brown Onion Soup

I have made this soup successfully, many times over the last 20 years, always using instant stock powders. The fact remains that you can't make onion soup without peeling and chopping onions. Still what are a few tears?

For 6–8 servings:

4–6 large onions
100g butter
2 tsp sugar
¼ cup flour
6 cups water
4 tsp instant beef stock powder
2 tsp chicken or vegetable stock powder
2 tsp Worcestershire sauce
¼ cup sherry
seasonings

Cheesy Croutons:

6–8 diagonal slices of French bread
½–1 cup grated Gruyere or tasty cheese

Halve the peeled onions and cut into 5mm slices. Melt the butter in a large heavy-bottomed pot, add the onions and cook over moderate heat, stirring frequently, for about 20 minutes, or until the onions have softened and browned. Do not hurry this step or the flavour will be spoilt.

Stir in the sugar, cook for about 5 minutes longer, until the mixture darkens more, then stir in the flour and cook about a minute longer.

Add the water 2 cups at a time, bringing the soup to the boil after each addition. Add the instant stock powders with the last amount of water, then simmer over a very low heat for 30 minutes.

Add the Worcestershire sauce and sherry, taste, then add freshly ground black pepper, a little more sugar and salt if required. Add a few drops of Tabasco sauce if you like.

Top each bowl with a freshly made cheesy crouton before serving.

To make the croutons, grill both sides of the sliced French bread until lightly browned. Pile the grated cheese on top and grill until the cheese melts.

HINTS: If you have the time, make this soup the day before you want it, since its flavour improves on standing.

Replace the water and instant stocks with homemade beef stock (page 58) if you like. Depending on the flavour of your stock, you will probably need to add extra salt.

This is a good soup to serve to departing guests after a late night party.

Swede Soup

Here is a slightly modified version of the original, popular Swede Soup I prepared on television many years ago. Do not consider swedes to be only "sheep food," since they give a surprising, unrecognisable flavour to this soup.

For 4 large servings:

2 bacon rashers

1 Tbsp olive oil or butter

1 onion

2 cloves garlic

½ carrot

½ celery stalk

400g swede

2 cups chicken stock*

1 tsp sugar

freshly ground black pepper

¼ tsp freshly grated nutmeg, optional

25g butter

2 Tbsp flour

1½ cups milk

½ – 1 tsp salt

2 Tbsp cream cheese, optional

about ¼ cup cream, optional

Remove the rind from the bacon, chop the rest finely, then cook with the rind in a large pot with the oil or butter.

Stir in the chopped onion, garlic, carrot and celery, cover and cook over a low heat for 5–10 minutes without browning.

While the vegetables "sweat", cut the peeled swede into pieces no bigger than 1cm cubes and add to the pot with the stock, sugar, ground pepper and nutmeg.

Simmer for 5–10 minutes, only until the swede is tender. (If you overcook the swede you spoil its flavour.)

Remove and discard the bacon rind, transfer the vegetables, with a little of the liquid to a food processor or blender, adding the cream cheese at this stage, if you choose, then puree until smooth. (Save the rest of the liquid.)

In another pot, melt the butter, add the flour and cook for 30 seconds, then add half the milk and bring to the boil, stirring all the time. When thick and smooth add the rest of the milk and the vegetable cooking liquid and stir until it thickens.

Add the swede puree and season carefully to taste. Add the cream to the thickened soup if desired.

Serve garnished with croutons (page 59), chopped parsley or spring onions or a spoonful of whipped cream and a sprinkling of paprika.

VARIATION: Instead of making the white sauce, use an extra ¼ cup of cream. This makes a smaller quantity of soup.

* Use homemade stock (pages 55–58) or 2 teaspoons of instant stock powder in 2 cups of water.

Roasted Corn Soup

Five years ago I would not have dreamed of roasting corn cobs before using them to make soup! This intensifies the fresh corn flavour and is one which we associate with late summer, and the pleasures of wayside stalls!

For 4 servings:

4 large corn cobs

25g butter

4 cloves garlic

1 red pepper, optional

1 large potato

4 cups chicken stock (page 56) or 4 tsp instant stock powder in 4 cups water

¼ cup cream

seasonings

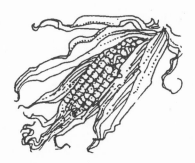

Pull back the husks from the corn cobs and remove the silk. Melt the butter and brush over the kernels then pull the husks back to cover the cobs again.

Place the corn cobs in one layer in a roasting pan with the whole, unpeeled garlic cloves, and the halved red pepper, and bake at 220°C for 20 minutes.

While the corn roasts, peel and roughly chop the potato and cook in a large pot with the chicken stock until the potato is tender.

Using a slotted spoon lift out the cooked potato and put in a food processor, blender or mouli.

Take the husks off the roasted corn cobs. With a sharp serrated knife, cut the kernels off the cobs, then scrape any remaining corn flesh from the cobs using a dessertspoon held bowl down.

Puree the kernels and flesh from three cobs with the potato, add the pulp squeezed from the garlic cloves, then return mixture to the pot with the chicken stock.

Finely dice the red pepper discarding the stem and seeds. Add to the soup with the corn cut from the last cob, and the cream, and bring to the boil. Adjust seasonings to suit your taste, adding a little salt, sugar, Tabasco sauce and freshly ground black pepper if necessary.

Reheat just before serving. Top individual servings with finely chopped parsley or coriander leaves.

VARIATIONS: Add a little chipotle powder, paste or sauce to the potatoes if you have it and like the idea of its subtle, smoky flavour in your soup.

Barbecue the corn, garlic (on a skewer) and the red pepper if preferred.

Corn & Bacon Chowder

This chunky chowder is substantial enough to serve for your main meal of the day. What's more, if you move fast, your chowder can be ready to eat 15 minutes after you walk into the kitchen.

For 4 large servings:

2 bacon rashers

1 onion or leek

1 Tbsp butter

1 carrot

1 potato

1 cup water

2 tsp instant bacon stock powder or 1 tsp
   salt

450g can whole kernel corn

1–1½ cups milk

50g butter

3 Tbsp flour

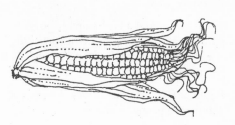

Cut the rinds off the bacon rashers, chop the rest finely then cook with the rind and the chopped onion or leek in a small frypan in the first measure of butter, for 4–5 minutes. Discard the rind.

Scrub and cut the carrot and potato into 1cm cubes, then cook in the water in a large pot for 10 minutes or until the vegetables are tender. Stir in the cooked bacon and onion (or leek).

Strain the liquid from the canned corn and make it up to 2 cups with milk.

In another pot or microwave dish, melt the second measure of butter and stir in the flour. When the mixture bubbles, add about ½ of the milk mixture. Stir frequently until boiling. Add the remaining milk, and cook until the sauce is smooth and thick.

Stir the sauce into the cooked vegetable mixture. Mash or puree if desired, then add the corn. Reheat before serving.

Serve with toast or crusty bread or rolls as a complete meal. Top with freshly chopped herbs if desired.

Corn & Bacon Chowder

Dot's Mysterious Beer Soup

Dot's Mysterious Beer Soup

Whenever I serve this soup, I am asked what is in it. My friends and family find the combination of carrots, cream cheese and lager delicious — but cannot identify the single flavours.

For 6 servings:

2 large onions
2 large carrots
25g butter
¼ cup flour
2 cups chicken stock (page 56) or 2 tsp
*   instant stock powder in 2 cups water*
250g carton cream cheese
1 can (about 2 cups) lager
chopped parsley

Chop finely or grate the onions and carrots.

Melt the butter in a large pot and add the onion. Cook over a low heat until very lightly browned and quite soft.

Add the grated carrots, cover and cook for 5–10 minutes longer, until the carrots are soft.

Stir in the flour and cook for another minute, then add the chicken stock. Stir over a gentle heat until the soup boils and thickens.

Remove from the heat and allow to cool slightly before pureeing, in several batches if necessary, in a food processor or blender. Pour back into the pot.

Put the cream cheese and lager in the (unwashed) food processor or blender and blend until smooth. Add this to the vegetable puree in the pot, and stir to combine. Reheat before serving.

Serve topped with finely chopped parsley or coriander leaves and cheesy pastry croutons or plain croutons (page 59).

Smooth & Crunchy Cream Soup

Although you may think that crunchy raw vegetables are a peculiar addition to hot soup, I hope that you will keep an open mind, because this creamy soup is as good hot as it is cold.

For 4 servings:

2 fairly large potatoes

2 cups milk

½–1 tsp finely chopped garlic

¼ tsp salt

½ cup cream cheese

¼ cup dry white wine

¼ cup cream

¼ cup each of chopped watercress, lettuce, spinach, grated cucumber

2 spring onions

¼ cup chopped snow pea sprouts

Peel and cube the potatoes. Put in a medium-sized pot with the milk, fresh or bottled minced garlic and the salt. Cover, and cook gently until the potatoes are tender.

Measure the cream cheese, wine and cream into a food processor or blender. Using a slotted spoon, transfer the hot cooked potato from the pot to the food processor or blender, and puree until smooth. Add the cooking liquid after potato is pureed.

If you want a very smooth soup, sieve the mixture after processing it. Taste and adjust seasonings if necessary, adding extra salt and freshly ground pepper.

Make sure that the vegetables you are going to add to the soup are fresh and crisp. Do not chop them in the food processor, since this may spoil their clean, fresh appearance. Prepare them just before the soup is to be served. Chop the leaves

finely (using a very sharp knife) and grate the cucumber on a sharp, hand held grater, holding the cucumber at right angles. (Do not use a very fine grater or you will finish up with pulp.) Thinly slice the spring onions and snow pea sprouts.

If serving the soup hot, heat it and stir in the vegetables seconds before you pour it into bowls.

If serving cold, make sure that the soup and the vegetables are well chilled. Combine them no more than 5 minutes before serving.

Sprinkle with croutons or serve with crostini or Melba toast (pages 59-60) before serving.

Curried Cashew & Carrot Soup

This is a delicious and unusual soup. It is filling and substantial. Its texture will vary with the way you toast and grind the cashew nuts. The finer the nuts are ground, the smoother and thicker the soup will be.

For 4 servings:

3 large (500g) carrots

2 small onions

1 Tbsp butter

1–2 Tbsp curry powder

3 cups chicken stock (page 56) or 2 tsp instant stock powder in 2 cups water

1 cup toasted cashew nuts

Slice the carrots thinly and chop the onions finely. Melt the butter in a medium-sized pot, add the curry powder and the chopped onions, cover and cook over medium heat, without browning, until the onions are soft.

Add the carrots and stock and simmer until the carrots are tender.

While the carrots cook, grind the roasted cashew nuts to the consistency of ground almonds in a food processor or blender. (If your cashews are not already roasted, place them under a grill in a shallow pan with ½ teaspoon of oil. Cook until golden brown, watching carefully that they do not burn, tossing occasionally.)

Lift the cooked carrots and onions out of their cooking liquid with a slotted spoon and place in the food processor or blender with the ground cashews. Process, adding just enough cooking liquid to moisten the mixture enough to form a smooth puree.

When smooth, add the remaining stock and process again.

To ensure that no chunky pieces remain, pour through a sieve if desired.

Taste and adjust seasoning if necessary.

Reheat before serving.

For extra flavour and contrast, mix together ½ cup of unsweetened plain yoghurt, 2 teaspoons of finely chopped mint or coriander leaves and 1 clove very finely chopped, or grated garlic. Swirl this into individual servings at the last minute.

VARIATION: This soup makes a good main dish for vegetarians if you use vegetable stock instead of chicken stock.

Mariners' Mussel Soup

Mussels are marvellous value for money! They are nutritious, full of flavour and are tender and succulent as long as you take care not to overcook and toughen them. Try this easy recipe and impress your guests!

For 4 servings:

1.5kg (about 24 fairly large) cultivated mussels
2 large onions
1 Tbsp olive or other oil
1 tsp finely chopped garlic*
pinch saffron, optional
½ cup white wine
425g can Savoury Tomatoes
chopped parsley or coriander leaves

Buy cultivated mussels from your supermarket the day you are going to cook and eat them. Do not choose mussels which are open or which have cracked or broken shells.

Scrub the live mussels, pulling out the beards and discarding any which do not close when tapped.

Chop the onions finely. Heat the oil in a large pan with a lid, and cook the onions and garlic until transparent, but not browned. Add saffron (if available), wine and the canned tomatoes.

Bring the mixture to the boil, add half the mussels and simmer with the lid on, until the shells open about 1cm. Watch carefully, turning the mussels so they heat evenly, lifting each mussel out with tongs as soon as it is ready.

Arrange the opened mussels in individual bowls, and keep in a warm place while you cook the remaining mussels.

The tomato mixture will be diluted by liquid from the mussels. This adds extra flavour. Boil the broth briskly for about 2 minutes, then spoon evenly over the mussels in the bowls. Sprinkle with chopped parsley or coriander leaves.

Serve with chunks of crusty bread to dip into the soup.

VARIATIONS: Substitute the Savoury Tomatoes with other seasoned canned tomatoes. Add a little chili powder to the onion and oil. Add herbs such as bayleaves to the cooking liquid.

HINT: To make sure you get maximum flavour and colour from saffron threads, grind them in a pestle and mortar before adding them to onion mixture.

* Use fresh or bottled garlic (see recipe on page 4).

Cream of Mussel Soup

Serve this creamy gourmet soup with pride! It has a lovely flavour, rather similar to that of oyster soup, but is cheap enough to serve often.

For 4 servings:

500–600g cultivated mussels
1 clove garlic, finely chopped
25g butter
3 Tbsp flour
½ tsp freshly grated nutmeg
mussel stock made up to 3 cups with milk
salt and pepper

Check mussels, discarding any which are cracked or which do not shut immediately if tapped.

Cook the mussels by steaming them in about ¼ cup of water in a covered pot or pan until they open. Remove the first to open with tongs, then cover again and steam the remainder. (If overcooked, they shrink and toughen.)

Strain the liquid from the pan, and make it up to 3 cups with milk.

In a clean pot, cook the finely chopped garlic in butter until straw-coloured. Stir in the flour and nutmeg and cook until bubbling, then add half the milk and stock mixture. Stir constantly over medium heat until the sauce thickens and boils, then add the rest of the liquid and bring back to the boil, stirring often. Simmer gently for 2–3 minutes, then remove from heat.

Chop the shelled mussels in a food processor, blender or mouli until pureed, adding some of the sauce from the pot to thin the puree. Pour, then push this through a sieve into the sauce, and discard the mussel solids.

Mix well and season to taste. Cool, then refrigerate if not serving immediately. Just before serving, gently reheat without boiling in a pot or microwave bowl. (Flavour is best after soup has stood for a few hours.)

For special occasions, swirl a spoonful of softly whipped cream into each bowl. Top with tiny croutons (page 59) or serve with crackers or toast.

Oyster Soup

This gourmet soup has, sadly, almost priced itself off our tables. Since you can make it with frozen oysters, or from oysters not quite fresh enough to serve raw, I think it is still worth including in this book.

For 4 servings:

18 oysters
75g butter
1–2 cloves garlic
1/2 tsp freshly grated nutmeg
1/4 cup flour
4–5 cups milk
juice of 1 lemon
salt and pepper

Drain the oysters saving their liquid.

Remove the beards from the oysters. (The beard is the frilly bit around the edge, and the clear piece next to the fleshy, most tender part.)

Put the beards in a medium-sized pot with the butter. Cook over a low heat for 5–10 minutes, taking care not to let the butter brown.

As the beards cook, add the chopped garlic and grated nutmeg. Stir in the flour and cook for 2 minutes longer.

Stir in the oyster liquid and 2 cups of milk. Keep stirring until the sauce thickens and boils. Add another cup of milk and bring back to the boil, stirring all the time. Put this in a food processor or blender with the fourth cup of milk, and process with the metal chopping blade until the beards are very finely chopped. (Process in 2 batches if necessary.)

Pour through a sieve back into the pot, discarding the pieces remaining in the sieve. Bring back to the boil, adding extra milk until the soup is the thickness that you like.

Slice the reserved oyster flesh and add to the soup with the lemon juice. Season carefully to taste.

For best flavour leave to stand for at least an hour before serving. Reheat, but do not boil at any time, after you have added the oysters.

Top with a spoonful of lightly whipped cream, and finely chopped chives or parsley, and serve with tiny croutons, Melba toast (page 59) or small crackers.

HINT: You get a stronger flavour when you puree the soup in a food processor before sieving it. Leave out this step if you do not have this equipment, however.

Shellfish Soup Supreme

You can make wonderful soup from freshly collected shellfish. Use one type, or several. (Always take care to find what limits have been enforced, and gather live shellfish from clean, unpolluted seashores.)

For 4 servings:

2–3 cups shelled tuatuas, pipis, etc
1 tsp finely chopped garlic
1 onion
1 tsp chopped thyme or dill leaves
1–2 bayleaves, optional
5cm strip lemon rind, optional
water or dry white wine
50g butter
¼ cup flour
¼–½ cup cream
salt and pepper

Open the shellfish by heating them in a large, covered frypan in a little water or unsalted fish stock (page 58), or microwave them a handful at a time in a covered dish, until the shells open. Save all liquid. (Do not worry about removing traces of sand, since this will not appear in your finished soup.)

Puree the shellfish meat with the garlic and onion in a food processor, blender or mouli, or chop it finely. Measure the puree and make up to 4 cups with the saved cooking liquid and water.

Simmer this in a medium-sized pot with the herbs and lemon rind for 20 minutes.

Strain through a cloth in a sieve or colander, squeezing the cloth to extract all liquid. Discard the solids. Make the liquid up to 5 cups with more water, unsalted fish stock or dry white wine if necessary. Put aside.

In a large pot melt the butter and cook gently with the flour for 2–3 minutes. Add the strained cooking liquid, 1 cup at a time, stirring after each addition until it boils again. Watch carefully to prevent burning on the bottom of the pot.

Remove from heat, add enough cream to "soften" its flavour, and adjust the seasonings carefully adding small amounts of salt, pepper, sugar, or Tabasco sauce if necessary.

Serve with crusty bread rolls for a casual meal, or serve at the beginning of a more formal meal, topped with lightly whipped cream, finely chopped fresh herbs or a sprinkling of paprika.

VARIATION: Be creative! I have tasted "imitation toheroa soup" made with much more mundane shellfish, coloured with pureed (babyfood) spinach, and named Bongo Bongo Soup!

Chunky Shrimp Chowder

This quickly made "meal in a bowl" is one of my favourites, because it tastes so good, as well as being quick and economical. Keep a can of shrimps in your store cupboard, so you can make it at short notice, for unexpected guests.

For 4 – 6 servings:

2 medium onions

2 stalks celery

25g butter

1 cup hot water

1 tsp instant green herb stock powder

1 tsp instant chicken stock powder

3 medium (450g) potatoes

about 1 cup frozen peas or mixed vegetables, optional

200g can shrimps

2 cups milk

about 2 Tbsp cornflour

parsley and paprika for garnish

Chop the onions and celery into 1cm chunks. Cook gently in the butter, in a large covered pot, until tender but not browned.

Add the water, instant stock powders, and the potatoes which have been scrubbed then cut into 1cm cubes. Cover and simmer for 15 minutes, or until potatoes are tender, adding the frozen vegetables (or mixed fresh vegetables) so they will be cooked at the same time as the potatoes.

When the potatoes are tender, add the shrimps, the liquid from the can, and the milk, then bring to the boil. Thicken with cornflour mixed to a paste with cold water, and adjust seasonings to taste.

TO MICROWAVE: You do not save much time by microwaving this chowder, but you do not need to stand over the pot as it cooks!

Heat the butter with the chopped onion and celery in a covered microwave dish on High (100% power) for 3–4 minutes, or until tender. Add boiling water, stock powders and the cubed potatoes, and cook for about 6 minutes, until the potatoes are tender. Add the rest of ingredients and 1 tablespoon of the cornflour, mixed to a paste with a little water, and heat until thick, for 7–10 minutes. Add remaining cornflour (mixed with water) if chowder is not thick enough. Heat through and serve.

Serve the chowder straight away or reheated, sprinkled with chopped parsley or dill sprigs and paprika, topped with a little sour cream if you have it.

VARIATION: Many people have told me that they make this chowder with canned salmon if they do not have shrimps. Since the flavour is much milder, use a much larger can.

Creamy Fish Chowder

This main-meal chowder is well worth the several steps involved, and is a good way to serve less expensive, whole fish, or better still, a fish which you have caught, but which you do not want to fillet.

For 4–6 servings:

1 large onion
2 stalks celery
1–2 carrots
3 Tbsp butter
1 cup water
2 tsp instant green herb or chicken stock
  powder
about ½ cup whole kernel corn
about ½ cup frozen peas
500–600g whole fish
½ cup white wine or water
3 Tbsp flour
1–2 cups milk

Slice the onion, celery and carrots and cook gently in 1 tablespoon of butter in a large covered pot for 3–4 minutes, without browning.

Add the water and instant stock powder and cook until the vegetables are tender, then add the corn and peas and cook a little longer.

In a large covered pot or pan, cook the whole or halved fish* in the water or wine until it flakes, then strain the liquid through a sieve into the vegetables.

Flake the fish, discarding skin and bones, and add the flaked fish to the pot with the vegetables.

Clean the pot or pan in which the fish cooked then melt the second measure of butter in it, and stir in the flour, heating until it bubbles. Add 1 cup of milk and bring to the boil, stirring constantly.

Strain in all the liquid from the fish and vegetables and cook until sauce is smooth and boiling, stirring all the time. Add extra milk or water if too thick. Simmer for about 5 minutes then gently stir in the fish and vegetables and check the seasoning.

Reheat carefully when ready to serve.

Garnish with fresh herbs and serve with garlic bread (page 60).

* The fish should be gutted, but need not have its skin or scales removed before cooking.

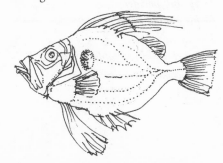

Shank Soup

This old-fashioned soup is packed full of cereals, pulses and vegetables and is very substantial. A large, two cup serving with a crusty bread roll makes a complete warming meal on a winter's evening.

For 5–6 servings:

2–3 lamb or hogget shanks
1 large onion
2–3 large cloves garlic
2 carrots
12 cups (3 litres) water
1/2 cup each barley, "soup mix" and split
    peas or brown lentils
1 tsp celery seed
1 tsp dried oreganum
1 tsp ground cumin
1/2 tsp dried thyme
1/8 tsp chili powder
freshly ground black pepper
1 1/2 tsp salt
3 cups chopped vegetables
1/2 cup chopped parsley

In a large pot brown the shanks, turning them several times while you chop the onion and garlic. Add the finely chopped onion and garlic, with a teaspoon of butter or oil, if no fat has come from the meat.

Cut the carrots into 1cm cubes and add to the browned shanks. Next add the water – it can be hot, cold or warm, but hot saves time – then everything else except the last 3 ingredients.

Cover the pot, leaving the lid ajar so it will not easily boil over, then simmer for 1 1/2 hours if you are in a hurry, or for 2 hours for maximum flavour.

Lift the shanks out of the soup and add the salt and a good selection of chopped raw vegetables, such as potato, kumara, pumpkin, cauliflower, cabbage, etc. to the soup.

While these cook, cut the meat off the shanks into chunky pieces. Return them to the soup. Discard any trimmings, but replace the bones in the soup if you like. (Remove these later, before you serve.) When the vegetables are tender, check the level of liquid, adding a few more cups of water if necessary. Simmer for a little longer, then adjust the seasonings carefully, add the chopped parsley and serve.

HINTS: On standing overnight, the soup may thicken, and need further thinning with extra water before you heat and serve it again. (Never leave soup standing overnight at room temperature, since it may ferment and spoil, even in cold weather.)

If you do not want to eat the whole batch of soup over the next few days, freeze it in several containers.

Barley Broth

This soup brings back memories of cold winter days, opening the door to a mother's welcome and the aroma of soup, getting a bowlful straight from the pot, and chatting by the fire while the soup "warmed the cockles of my heart".

For 12 or more servings:

1 large bag (about 2kg) soup bones
water to cover
3 large onions
3 stalks celery
3 large carrots
3 large cloves garlic
1 tsp black peppercorns
1 cup barley

3–4 cups finely chopped vegetables
fresh herbs, optional
1 cup chopped parsley

Place the bones in a very large pot and cover them with water. (If you prefer a browner soup, place the bones in a large roasting dish and grill or roast them in a very hot oven, until the edges and rough bits turn dark brown and char, before putting them in the pot with the water.)

Chop the onions and add to the pot, skin, roots and all. Add the roughly chopped celery, scrubbed carrots, peeled garlic and peppercorns.

Place the barley in a large sieve and lower the sieve into the pot so it will be immersed in the stock. Cover the pot and simmer very slowly for 4 or 5 hours. (This allows you to lift out the barley before you strain the stock and discard the bones and vegetables.)

Remove the pot from the heat, then take out and put aside the sieve of barley. Strain the stock, discard the bones and vegetables, and put the stock back in the pot. Skim the fat from the top.

Put the barley back in the stock, add a mixture of whatever finely chopped vegetables you like and your favourite chopped fresh herbs, and simmer about 30 minutes or until the vegetables are tender. Add salt and freshly ground pepper to taste during the last 15 minutes of cooking. (You will probably need to add several teaspoons of salt, since this is a large quantity of soup.)

Store cooled soup in covered containers in the refrigerator, for 2–3 days, reheating as much as you need each time. For longer storage, freeze soup in airtight plastic containers.

Serve topped with finely chopped parsley, with crusty bread.

Granny's Chicken Soup

Old fowls make wonderful soup, so it is worth hunting them down if you are a serious soup maker! You will find these "retired layers" at some supermarkets, at Asian food suppliers, in some butchers' shops and egg farms.

For 6–8 servings:

1 (about 1.5kg) "roasting fowl" or "roasting hen"

8 cups (2 litres) water

1–2 tsp finely chopped garlic*

1 tsp grated or minced fresh ginger*

2 Tbsp soya sauce

2 Tbsp sherry

1 onion

1 carrot

1 stalk celery

½ cup macaroni

1 Tbsp rolled oats

1 small potato

chopped parsley and other fresh herbs

salt and pepper

Thaw the bird if necessary, remove neck and giblets from body cavity and place the bird, giblets etc in a pot which will hold the bird and the water. Add to the chicken and water the next 4 ingredients.

Cover tightly and bring to the boil, then simmer gently for about 4 hours, adding the tops, bottoms and any peelings from the onion, carrot and celery, as soon as the you prepare these vegetables which are to be added later.

Lift the bird from the pot, and when cool enough to work with separate the flesh from the skin and bones, using your fingers. Put all the bones and trimmings back to cook in the liquid for 30–60 minutes longer.

Strain off the liquid and discard the debris. Pour, spoon or skim off the fat which rises to the top.

To make the soup, bring the stock back to the boil, add the finely chopped onion, carrot and celery and bring back to the boil before adding the macaroni and rolled oats.

Simmer for 20–30 minutes or until the macaroni and vegetables are tender, then add the grated unpeeled potato, chopped herbs and season carefully to taste. (The potato will thicken the soup and must not be added before the other vegetables are cooked.)

Add some of the cold chopped chicken if you like.

Serve with dumplings (page 60). Refrigerate or freeze leftovers.

HINT: Soup left to stand for long, may need to be thinned down with vegetable cooking liquid or water. Adjust seasoning before serving.

* Use fresh, or from the jars described at the end of the recipe on page 4.

Kirsten's Quick Soup

This quickly made family soup is easy enough for children to make for themselves, in 15 minutes. The quantities given here may be varied but the order of additions is important and should not be changed.

For 4 servings:

4 cups hot water
4 tsp instant chicken stock powder
1 tsp sugar
2 tsp butter
½ cup small curly-edged lasagne noodles
1 small onion
1 stalk celery
1 small carrot
1 small potato
1 tomato
1 Tbsp chopped parsley

Put the hot water and instant stock powder into a medium-sized pot over a high heat.

Add the sugar and butter.

When this comes to the boil, add the lasagne noodles. Bring back to the boil then turn down the heat so the soup is simmering.

Prepare the vegetables, in the order given, adding each as it is ready.

Quarter the onion then remove its skin. Cut it into very thin slices.

Cut the celery into very thin (2mm) slices.

Scrub then grate the carrot.

Scrub or thinly peel the potato, then grate it.

Cut the tomato into small (5mm) cubes.

The soup should be cooked about 10 minutes after the noodles are added, but it needs to cook for 3–5 minutes after the potato is added.

Stir in the chopped parsley and serve, straight away, or reheat later.

This soup goes well with garlic bread (page 60), toasted cheese sandwiches or bread rolls.

VARIATION: If you have it, use homemade vegetable, chicken or beef stock instead of the water and instant stock powder.

Minestrone

This soup is colourful and popular. It is made from stock with added tomatoes and is filled with vegetables, beans and pasta. You can make it very quickly if you start with precooked (canned) beans and frozen or instant stock.

For 6 servings:

1 large onion, carrot and celery stalk
2 Tbsp olive or other oil
½ tsp finely chopped garlic
4 cups chicken, beef or vegetable stock*
400g can tomatoes in juice
¼ cup macaroni
1 cup chopped zucchini
1 cup chopped green beans
1 cup chopped cabbage
1 can kidney beans
sugar, pepper and salt to taste
freshly chopped herbs
Parmesan cheese

Chop the onion, carrot and celery into small cubes and cook in the oil in a large pot for about 15 minutes or until the onion is tender and the vegetables are lightly browned.

Stir in the garlic and cook a few seconds longer.

Add the stock and the tomatoes, squashing them to break them up if necessary.

Bring to the boil then add the macaroni and cook for a few minutes while you prepare the green vegetables. Add these, bring back to the boil and simmer for a few minutes longer before adding the canned beans. (It is not critical what size can or colour of bean that you add, so use what you think will look and taste best. You can also add the liquid from the beans if you like.)

Cook gently for a few minutes after the last addition, then taste and adjust the seasonings, adding a little sugar to intensify the tomato flavour. Add any finely chopped herbs that you like.

Serve immediately or reheat, topping individual servings with grated Parmesan cheese.

* Use homemade stock (pages 55–58), bought ready prepared liquid stock, or 4 teaspoons of instant stock powder in 4 cups of water.

Pea Soup with Bacon

Since pea soup contains a high proportion of legumes I consider it a meal in itself when I serve it topped with a few slices of sizzling sausage. These add interest in flavour and texture too, and always seem popular with children.

For 8–10 servings:

250–500g bacon pieces
2 large onions
2–3 stalks celery
2 medium carrots
1 tsp finely chopped garlic
8–10 cups (2–2.5 litres) water
¾ cup split yellow peas
½ cup red lentils
3 Tbsp butter
¼ cup flour
milk, water or stock to thin
salt and pepper

Remove the rind from the bacon pieces and chop them finely. Brown, adding a little oil if necessary, in the pot in which the soup is to be cooked. Add the coarsly chopped vegetables and garlic and cook for 2–3 minutes, then add the water, peas and lentils.

Cover, but leave the lid ajar, and cook for about 2 hours (or 30 minutes in a pressure cooker), until the peas are tender. (Use the smaller amount of water if the soup is pressure cooked.)

Puree in batches in a food processor, blender or mouli.

Rinse out the pan and melt the butter in it. Add the flour, cook briefly, then add a cup of the pureed mixture. Bring to the boil, stirring constantly, then add another cup of the mixture and bring back to the boil. Add the remaining puree, bring to the boil again, and simmer for 5 minutes.

The resulting soup is very thick. I store it in jars in the refrigerator or in cartons in the freezer, and thin it as I use it with milk, water or stock. (The amount of these depends on the thickness you want.)

Taste the soup critically after thinning it and adjust the seasonings. The amount of salt required depends on saltiness of the bacon. Add freshly ground pepper to taste.

Serve very hot, garnished with slices of cooked sausage browned in a little oil in a frypan, with crumbled cooked bacon, or croutons (page 59).

Lentil Soup with Coriander Leaves

This soup is made from basic, inexpensive ingredients, contains no meat or stock, but tastes very good indeed. Dress it up for a special occasion, serving it with bowls of colourful and tasty extras, so your guests can add whatever they like.

For 8–10 servings:

1½ cups brown/green lentils
10 cups (2.5 litres) water
2 bayleaves, optional
2 small dried chilis

¼ cup olive or other oil
2 large onions
3–4 stalks celery
1 green pepper
4 cloves garlic
1 tsp dried oreganum
1 tsp ground cumin
2 Tbsp finely chopped coriander leaves
3 Tbsp wine vinegar (red for preference)
about 1 tsp salt
black pepper

Simmer together in a large pot the lentils, water, bayleaves and chilis, for 45–60 minutes, or until lentils are very soft. (Lentils which have been presoaked will be tender in 20 minutes.)

While the lentils cook, heat the oil in a large frypan. Add the onions, celery and pepper, all cut in small pieces about the size of the lentils.

Cook without browning for about 10 minutes, then leave to stand.

While both the above mixtures are cooking, chop the garlic and add half to the pot with the lentils, and half to the mixture in the pan. Add half the oreganum and cumin to each container, in the same way.

When the lentils are soft, tip the mixture from the frypan into the lentils, bring to the boil and simmer 15 minutes longer.

Remove from the heat, take out the bayleaves and chilis, add the chopped coriander leaves and vinegar, then add salt and freshly ground black pepper to taste.

Serve immediately or reheat when needed.

A lovely addition to this soup is a simple salsa. Prepare a bowl of chopped, blanched, seeded tomatoes, (preferably Italian tomatoes if you can get them), spring onion leaves and chopped coriander leaves, so diners can add a generous spoonful of this to their soup just before eating it.

Other optional last-minute additions include sliced cooked sausages, chopped ham, crumbled crisp bacon, croutons, salsa or pesto (page 61), grated Parmesan cheese, and sour cream. A selection of these, arranged in small bowls on a tray, turns this soup into a party meal.

Lentil Soup with Coriander Leaves

Mediterranean Bean Soup

Mediterranean Bean Soup

To most of us, "Mediterranean" means a blazing sun in a clear blue sky, and sparkling blue sea. This soup, however, is eaten in the cold Mediterranean winter, when it is just as welcome as it is here in nasty wet weather.

For 8 servings:

1½ cups haricot or baby lima beans
10 cups (2.5 litres) water
2–3 cloves garlic
2–3 bayleaves
2 large onions
2 carrots
2–3 stalks celery
400g can whole tomatoes in juice
1½ tsp salt
¼ cup olive oil
pepper
3–4 Tbsp freshly chopped parsley

Soak the dried beans in the water overnight. Pour off and measure the soaking water and replace with the same volume of fresh water.

Add the chopped garlic and the bay leaves and simmer for about half an hour. Chop and add the onions, carrots and celery and simmer for 30 minutes longer, until the beans are very soft. (If you want a thicker soup, puree all or half of the solids in the soup.) Add the tomato juice and chopped tomatoes, the salt, olive oil, plenty of pepper and the chopped parsley.

Leave to stand for a few hours for best flavour, then adjust the seasonings, adding about a teaspoon of brown sugar if needed. Remove the bay leaves.

Serve with crusty, solid bread. Slightly sour Italian bread is a delicious choice.

VARIATIONS: For a half-hour soup, pressure cook the beans, water, garlic and bayleaves for 20 minutes, add the vegetables and pressure-cook for 5 minutes.

For another very good soup with quite a different (but not Mediterranean) character, leave out the olive oil, puree all the solids, thicken with a tablespoon of cornflour mixed to a paste with cold water, and add ¼–½ cup of cream, or 2 tablespoons of butter.

a comforting soup for winter lunch.

Red Lentil, Carrot & Kumara Soup

Because lentils are the smallest members of the pulse family, they cook fastest, without soaking, so you can make a tasty soup, substantial enough for dinner on a cold night, in just over half an hour, making variations to suit your taste.

For 4–6 large servings:

1 large onion
2 Tbsp olive oil or butter
1 tsp finely chopped garlic
¼–½ tsp chili powder
2 tsp ground cumin
1 tsp freshly ground coriander seed
1 tsp turmeric
4 cups vegetable or chicken stock*
¾ cup red lentils
2 medium carrots
2 stalks celery
1 large kumara
¼–½ cup cream, optional
salt and freshly ground black pepper

Chop the onion into 1cm chunks and cook over low to moderate heat in the oil or butter for about 5 minutes. As it cooks, stir in the next 5 ingredients. Spices should smell fragrant, without burning.

Add the liquid and the lentils, bring to the boil and leave simmering while you add the carrots and celery cut in 5mm slices, and the thinly peeled kumara in 1cm cubes. Simmer the mixture, with the lid ajar, for 15–20 minutes, or until the lentils and vegetables are tender.

Puree all or part of the soup, depending on the texture you like. Thin with extra stock or water if very thick. Add cream to taste if you like. Taste and season to balance the flavours.

Top with pesto (page 61) or salsa (pages 40 or 61) if desired, and serve with crostini, garlic bread (page 60) or crusty bread rolls.

VARIATIONS: A few minutes before serving, stir into the soup pieces of cooked chicken, chopped ham or cooked bacon, or cubes of tofu.

Sprinkle Parmesan cheese on individual servings.

Replace kumara with potatoes.

(Made with oil and vegetable stock, without the cream, this soup is suitable for vegans.)

* Use homemade stock if possible, (pages 55–58) otherwise 4 teaspoons instant stock powder in 4 cups of water.

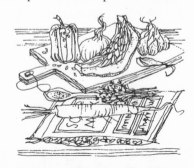

Creamy Lentil & Vegetable Soup

This is an excellent main meal soup that you can sit down to eat half an hour after you start to make it. You can change the ingredients, depending on the bits and pieces you have in the refrigerator, so it is never the same twice.

For 4–6 servings:

1 cup red lentils
25g butter
1 or 2 onions
1 or 2 cloves garlic
1 or 2 carrots
1 or 2 stalks celery
1 tsp whole or ground cumin seeds
½ tsp freshly ground coriander, optional
½ tsp each garam masala and paprika
2–4 Tbsp cream
2 Tbsp cornflour
1 cup frozen peas
about 1 cup chopped tomato
1 Tbsp sugar, optional
1–1½ tsp salt
about ¼ cup chopped fresh herbs

As soon as you think about making this soup, measure the lentils and 1 litre of hot tap water into a bowl or jug so that the lentils start softening.

Melt the butter in a large pot. Add the chopped onions, garlic, carrots and celery. If you intend to purée all or part of the soup, you can leave the vegetables in large pieces. If you want the soup unpuréed and fairly chunky, cut them into small even pieces.

Add the cumin, coriander, garam masala and paprika to the vegetables. (Leave out any of these which you do not have, or add 1–2 teaspoons curry powder, if you have none of them.)

Cook over moderate heat, stirring occasionally, for 2–3 minutes longer, without letting the vegetables brown.

Add the lentils and hot water, cover, and simmer for about 20 minutes, or until the vegetables and lentils are tender.

Purée all, or part, or none of the mixture, and bring it back to the boil.

Mix as much cream as you like to a paste with the cornflour and a little extra water, and pour into the soup.

Add the peas (or other frozen vegetables) and the tomato which has been chopped into pieces the same size as the peas.

Add the sugar, salt to taste and the fresh herbs. If you have any left-over cooked vegetables, cut them into small cubes and add them too. Simmer five minutes longer.

Serve sprinkled with Parmesan cheese if you like, with hot toast, croutons (page 59), or crusty bread.

Senate Bean Soup

This smooth and lovely soup is pale in colour, with a good flavour. Be very careful when you season something like this - too much salt leaves you feeling terribly thirsty later, but too little makes it bland and flavourless.

For about 10 servings:

2 ½ cups (400g) haricot beans
10 cups (2.5 litres) water
1 bacon hock*
1 tsp finely chopped garlic
2 onions
1 tsp celery seed
2 bayleaves, optional
1 small dried chili
salt and pepper to taste

Replace hock with about 200g of smoky bacon, in a chunk (a bacon end) or cut in pieces, if preferred.

Measure the beans into a large soup pot, and pick out any discoloured ones. Either pour water over them and leave to stand overnight, or pour boiling water over them and leave to stand for an hour.

When you are ready to start cooking the soup, add the bacon hock and the garlic, chopped onions and celery seed, the whole bayleaves and the chili.

Cover the pot, but leave the lid ajar, and simmer for 1½–2 hours, or until the bacon hock meat and beans are very tender. (If the bacon hock starts to fall apart before the beans are tender, lift it out – if the beans are tender before the bacon hock is tender, you just have to keep cooking them if you want to cube the bacon in your soup. If you want only the bacon flavour, take the bacon hock out as soon as the beans are very soft.) Overcooking does not hurt the soup, but undercooked beans spoil it completely.

Remove the cooked bacon hock, take off the skin and discard it, and chop the meat into cubes. Take out and discard the bayleaves and chili.

Puree the beans and onions with the cooking liquid, then add the cubed meat if you like pieces of it in the soup.

Check the texture. You can leave it as it is, make it smoother and thicker by adding a little cornflour mixed to a paste with cold water, or you can add cream to taste, or some cornflour and some cream. Season carefully with salt and pepper.

Serve in large bowls, topped with a knob of butter and a sprinkling of chopped parsley, or topped with a spiral of cream and a sprinkling of paprika, chives or parsley. For good texture contrast, serve some type of really crunchy bread with it. Read the possibilities on pages 59, 60, and 61.

Black Bean & Rice Soup

The dark colour of this soup is unusual, to say the least! Sour cream or yoghurt swirled on top, a sprinkling of chopped spring onions, and hot red pepper sauce or red tomato salsa make it look quite dramatic, and as good as it tastes.

For 4 main course servings:

1 cup small black (Tiger) beans

3 cups water

3 cups chicken, vegetable or beef stock (pages 55–58) or 3 tsp instant stock powder in 3 cups water

3 large onions

4 cloves garlic

2 Tbsp olive or other oil

2–3 tsp ground cumin

2 tsp dried oreganum

about 2 cups cooked brown rice

2 Tbsp wine vinegar

Simmer the beans in the first measure of water in a large pot until they are very tender and most of the water is absorbed. Add the stock, or the second measure of water and the instant stock powder. Simmer until the beans will break up easily. (These processes together should take 1–1½ hours. Cook longer if necessary, however.)

Meanwhile, chop the onions and garlic finely, with a food processor if available, and cook in the oil over low to moderate heat, in a medium-sized frypan, for 10–15 minutes, or until the onions are a pale golden colour but not brown. Add the cumin and oreganum after about 5 minutes.

Remove from the heat and mix in the cooked rice and the vinegar. (Replace half the vinegar with balsamic vinegar if you have it.)

When the beans are mushy, puree 1½ cups of them with enough of their cooking stock to make a thick liquid. Then combine the pureed and whole beans and stock, and the onion mixture.

Bring to the boil, taste, and season with Tabasco sauce, ground black pepper and salt. Add extra cumin and oreganum if the soup seems bland.

Serve immediately or reheat when required, thinning with more stock if it thickens too much on standing.

Serve each large bowl of soup topped with sour cream, yoghurt, or a mixture of the two, chopped spring onion leaves, and a little more Tabasco sauce or the salsa on pages 40 or 61. Put more of all the toppings on the table if you like.

Tomato Soup with Orange

There are often evenings in summer or early autumn when soup made from the ripest, reddest tomatoes in our garden is welcome. I serve the soup chilled or hot. A little orange makes it interesting and different, but it is not essential.

For 4 servings:

600g tomatoes

1 small onion

2 tsp olive oil

¼ cup white wine

2 cups chicken stock (page 56–57) or 2 tsp instant chicken stock powder in 2 cups water

1 orange, rind and juice

2 tsp wine vinegar or Balsamic vinegar

1 thick slice white bread

6 drops Tabasco sauce

¼–½ tsp salt

about 1 tsp sugar

freshly ground black pepper

To skin the tomatoes, pour boiling water over them, in a bowl. Leave for 1–2 minutes, until the skin will peel off easily. Halve the tomatoes, shake and squeeze out most of the watery part and seeds, then chop the flesh quite finely.

Cook the finely chopped onion in the oil until soft but not browned. Add the cubed tomatoes, wine and stock or water and stock powder and simmer gently for about 5 minutes.

Meantime, if you want an added orange flavour, finely grate the coloured rind from half an orange. If you want an orange rind garnish, cut a few small, thin strips of rind from the other side of the orange, using an orange zester, and put these aside. Put the grated rind in a bowl or shallow plate with the juice of the orange.

Add the piece of bread, and the vinegar. (If you are not adding the orange, add a little soup liquid to the bread.) When the bread has softened, mash it to a pulp with a fork, then stir this mixture into the hot soup. Add the remaining seasonings, checking to balance the flavours as you do this.

If soup is to be served cold, chill it for several hours. To cool it quickly, stand the pot in cold water containing a lot of ice-blocks.

Decorate the hot or cold soup with a small amount of the reserved orange zest.

Gazpacho

I never know how to describe Gazpacho. Is it a cold soup full of salad, or a salad in a soupy sort of dressing? Maybe I should just explain it as a cross between a salad and a soup, a wonderful starter for a summer meal or barbecue!

For 6 servings:

3 slices wholemeal or white bread

1kg ripe red tomatoes

5–6cm length of telegraph cucumber

3 Tbsp wine vinegar

2–3 Tbsp olive oil

1–2 cloves garlic

1 tsp sugar

2 tsp salt

1 Tbsp tomato paste

about 1 cup water

fresh basil or coriander leaves

Soak the bread in cold water, squeeze to extract most of the moisture, then mash with a fork until broken up.

Peel the tomatoes by holding over a gas flame or standing them in boiling water for a minute, then in cold water. Halve them, then shake out and discard the seeds and surrounding watery liquid before chopping them.

Grate the peeled cucumber and mix with the finely chopped tomatoes. Add the bread, vinegar and olive oil. Mash or puree the garlic with the sugar and salt and mix in well. Stir in the tomato paste. Add the water if the mixture looks and tastes too concentrated, otherwise leave it out.

Add a few chopped basil or coriander leaves, adjust the seasonings (tomato mixtures often need extra sugar) and chill for at least an hour.

Prepare small dishes of each of the following, allowing at least a spoonful of each for every diner:

chopped red, yellow and green peppers, cubed cucumber, chopped red onions, small croutons (page 59), diced avocado, pesto (page 61), chopped basil, or coriander leaves.

Serve the chilled gazpacho in bowls which contain one or two ice cubes, and pass around the bowls of additions, so that your friends and family can help themselves.

White Gazpacho with Grapes

If you like tomato-based gazpacho, I hope you will try this cold summer soup. When a friend extolled its virtues, I thought it sounded rather strange, and may not have tried it if she had not made it for me! I love it, and now make it every summer.

For 6 servings:

4 slices day-old bread
2 cloves garlic
1½ tsp salt
1 cup (100g) ground almonds
½ cup olive oil
¼ cup wine vinegar
4 cups iced water
about 50 green seedless grapes
ice-blocks
croutons

Choose bread with some body and character, rather than regular supermarket bread, if possible. Remove the crusts from the bread and soak in cold water.

Squeeze to extract most of the moisture, then put the bread into a food processor or blender, add the peeled garlic cloves, salt and ground almonds and blend this mixture to a smooth, thick paste. (The garlic will be chopped up much more efficiently in a thick paste than it is in a thin mixture.)

With the motor running, pour in the oil in a thin stream, as you would when making mayonnaise. Add the vinegar, then add one cup of the iced water.

Transfer to a large bowl and stir in the remaining 3 cups of water. Chill, up to 24 hours.

Serve the soup very cold in bowls, before the main course of dinner. Into each serving put about 8 halved grapes and one or two iceblocks, and let your friends and/or family help themselves to as many crisp, small croutons (page 59) as they like.

Wonton Soup

Shank Soup

Yoghurt & Cucumber Soup

Cucumber and yoghurt mixtures make good, quickly made, fresh tasting, low calorie soups, sauces and dressings, usually flavoured with mint, garlic and dill or coriander leaves. Experiment, to see if you like the flavours mixed or separate.

For 4 small servings:

2–3 telegraph cucumbers
1 tsp salt
2–3 spring onions
12–20 mint leaves
1–2 cloves garlic
1 large sprig parsley or several coriander
    sprigs
1 sprig dill, optional
2 cups plain unsweetened yoghurt
2 Tbsp cream, optional

Make sure that you use cucumbers which have thin, tender skins, and small, immature seeds. Halve the cucumbers lengthwise, and scoop out the seeds by running a teaspoon from one end to the other, along the central, seedy area. Discard the seeds.

Grate the remaining cucumber flesh, sprinkle with salt and leave to stand for 5–10 minutes.

Finely chop the flavourings which you have decided to use. (The food processor does this job efficiently. First process them without any liquid, then add a little yoghurt and process again.)

Squeeze the salted cucumber to remove excess liquid, and combine it with the seasonings and the remaining yoghurt. Add a little cream for extra richness, if you can justify it!

I think that the soup is nice with some cucumber pieces for texture, but if you like the idea of a smoother mixture, process again, until you have a pale green smooth mixture instead of a white one flecked with cucumber skin and herbs.

Taste and adjust the seasonings to suit your taste. (You can add spices such as cumin and a little hotness with chili paste or Tabasco sauce, if you like.)

Chill for at least 30 minutes, or up to 8 hours, before serving in small soup bowls, cups or glasses.

HINT: Low or no-fat yoghurt may be used successfully for this soup, but it does taste richer if a little cream is present.

Avocado Soup

If you have well-flavoured, ripe avocados on hand, it is worth making this quick, velvet-smooth soup. Use my recipe as a guide, making your own variations. Don't add very strong seasonings though, or you will lose the avocado flavour.

For 2–3 servings:

1–2 ripe avocados
1–2 Tbsp lemon juice
1 cup chicken stock (page 56–57) or 1 can
    Cream of Chicken Soup
water if necessary
2 tsp chopped spring onion
1–4 Tbsp fresh or sour cream, optional
Tabasco sauce

Make this easy soup no more than 15 minutes before you plan to serve it, since avocados darken on prolonged standing.

Halve the avocados, twist to separate the halves, then chop a sharp knife into the stones and twist to remove them from the flesh. Scoop the avocado flesh into a food processor bowl or blender, making sure you use all the darker green flesh close to the skin. (Do not use darker or blemished parts.)

Process, adding the lemon juice to slow down discolouration, then add the chicken stock or canned soup. If soup is thick, use only part of the can, and thin down your soup with water.

Add the finely chopped spring onion, (or coriander leaves or other fresh herbs) taste, season if necessary, then add a little fresh or sour cream and Tabasco sauce until it is exactly as you like it.

Depending on the thickness of the puree or soup, scoop it up with corn chips or crusty bread or use a spoon.

HINTS: If you must make this ahead, cover the surface with cling wrap. It will probably stand for an hour or so before discolouring, as long as you have added the lemon juice.

For an attractive appearance, swirl a little cream onto the surface of the soup or top with a spoonful of salsa (pages 40 or 61).

Although it is usual to serve this soup cold, you may like to try it hot, (but not boiling), at room temperature, and chilled, to see which option you like best.

If you are using a canned soup, make sure that it has a good flavour. If not, it will spoil your soup. You can't make a silk purse out of a sow's ear!

Stocks for Soups

Many soups need the addition of stock for added body, and to bring out the full flavour of other ingredients. You can choose from home-made stocks, bought liquid stocks, or instant stock powders and cubes. Each has its pros and cons.
I feel that frozen, home-made stocks are the best option for cooks who are really serious about soups, and want the best product for a low price, but instant stocks certainly have their place for anyone short of time, with a number of mouths to feed.
Read the whole of this section, then choose the stock which best suits your time, money and inclination!

Quick Vegetable Stock

Well flavoured vegetable stock may be made in 30 minutes if you start with very finely chopped vegetables.

For 3–4 cups:
1 large or 2 small onions
3 cloves garlic
1 large or 2 small carrots
1–2 stalks celery
1 Tbsp tomato paste
1 sprig parsley
1 sprig oreganum, or ½ tsp dried
1 tsp crushed black peppercorns
1 dried chili
1 bay leaf
4 cups water
1 tsp sugar
about 1 tsp salt

Quarter the unpeeled onions. Put in a food processor bowl with the unpeeled garlic cloves, the unpeeled carrot cut into chunks, and the roughly chopped celery stalks. Process finely, using the metal chopping blade, or chop finely by hand.

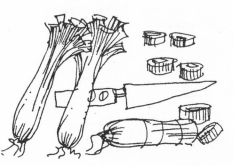

Transfer the chopped vegetables to a large pot, and add the remaining ingredients and simmer for 20–30 minutes then pour through a sieve, squeezing out as much liquid as possible.

Refrigerate up to 2 days or freeze up to 6 months.

Browned Vegetable Stock

For vegetable stock with a stronger flavour and colour, slightly modify the recipe above.

Chop the onion, carrots and celery in 5mm cubes and brown in about 1 tablespoon of butter or oil for 10–15 minutes, or until vegetables are evenly browned (but not black) then proceed as for Quick Vegetable Stock.

Stocks for Soups

Home-made Chicken Stock

Home-made chicken stock, frozen in 2 cup containers, is a wonderful ingredient to have on hand. It gives body and flavour to soups and sauces for very little cost. There are several different ways to make it.

Stock From Raw Chicken

I freeze raw chicken trimmings and giblets (except livers which make bitter stock) in a bag in my freezer, adding to the bag until it is full. Alone, or with fresh chicken backs bought specially, they make good stock, as long as other flavourings are added.

For 8 cups:

about 1kg of raw chicken bones, chicken
    backs, skin, giblets, feet etc.
1 tsp finely chopped garlic
1 onion, chopped
2 – 3 bay leaves
about 12 peppercorns
4 whole cloves
12 cups (3 litres) water
1 tsp dried oreganum, crumbled
1 tsp fresh or dried thyme
¼ cup coarsely chopped parsley
salt and pepper

Simmer whatever chicken bits you have, with everything except the salt and pepper in a very large pot, for 3 hours.

Strain though a sieve and discard the solids. Skim off and discard the fat from the surface.

Season to taste and refrigerate up to 2–3 days or freeze for up to 6 months.

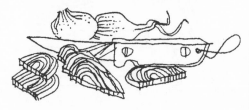

Stock From a Boiling Fowl

When you boil an old hen, you get stock with a much more intense chicken flavour, for a very low price. Look for frozen birds with labels such as Pot Roasters, Table Hens, or Roasting Fowls (at a fraction of the price of younger birds) at Asian Food Stores, some supermarkets and butchers, and some egg producers.

Put the thawed hen to simmer for 4–5 hours in 8 cups of water with a teaspoon each of finely chopped (or bottled) garlic and ginger, and 2 tablespoons each of soya sauce and sherry. (See details on page 36.) Spoon the fat from the top of the stock before refrigerating or freezing.

Chicken Bones Stock

The skeleton and other remains of roast, barbecued, grilled or baked chicken may be used to make useful, small amounts of good stock. Start cooking the stock while you do the dishes, while you still have the bones, drippings and vegetable trimmings from dinner close at hand.

Stocks for Soups

For 2–4 cups:

Cooked carcass, chicken bones, giblets,
*   skin, fat, etc.*
1–2 cloves garlic
1 carrot
1 onion
1 stalk celery, optional
1 Tbsp light soya sauce
½ tsp salt
6 peppercorns or 1 dried chili
water to cover

Put all the chicken remains in a fairly large pot, with any cooking juices scraped from the original cooking pan, and any suitable vegetable trimmings. Add the ingredients listed, cover and simmer for about 2 hours.

Strain off stock and refrigerate for short storage or freeze in covered containers for up to 6 months.

Chicken Giblet Stock

Giblets (available from many supermarkets) make quite a strongly flavoured stock with minimum cost, mess and effort.

For 8 cups:

500g chicken giblets
1–2 cloves garlic
1–2 slices fresh ginger, optional
1 Tbsp light soya sauce
1 Tbsp sherry
freshly ground black pepper
8 cups (2 litres) water

Put everything in a large pot and simmer for about 3 hours. Strain, reserving the cooked giblets to chop and add to soups before serving if you like.

Refrigerate stock for up to 3 days, or freeze for up to 6 months.

Fish Stock

Fish stock requires only a short cooking time. When you make it, open the window so the odours are quickly dispersed. (Use chicken stock for fish soups if you have no fish stock available.)

For 3–4 cups:

about 750g fish skeletons and/or fish heads
1 onion, sliced
1–2 cloves garlic
1 stalk celery, chopped
1 bay leaf
1 sprig parsley
1 sprig thyme
6 peppercorns or 1 dried chili
2–3cm strip lemon rind
4 cups water

Put everything in a fairly large pot. Bring to the boil, cover and simmer for 30 minutes, then strain through a fine

sieve and discard the solids. Refrigerate for 2–3 days or freeze in covered containers for up to 6 months.

HINT: Fresh salmon trimmings make excellent stock if they are available.

Brown Beef Stock

Although you can make stock from any beef bones, bones which contain marrow are generally regarded as best.

For about 10 cups:

1–2kg beef bones, cut into small sections
2–3 onions
2 carrots
2 stalks celery, optional
2 cloves garlic
1–2 bay leaves
10 peppercorns
1 tsp salt
½ tsp dried thyme
½ tsp dried oreganum
several parsley stalks, optional
about 12 cups (3 litres) cold water

For a good brown colour and the best flavour, heat the bones and the roughly chopped vegetables under a grill or in a very hot oven until the edges char. Turn bones and vegetables so they brown on both sides.

Transfer bones and vegetables to a very large pot, add the flavourings and water, cover and simmer for 4 – 5 hours.

Sieve the stock and leave to stand in a cool place until the fat rises to the surface and solidifies. Remove fat and refrigerate up to 2–3 days or freeze up to 6 months.

Beef Stock

If you do not have the time to brown bones, cook all the above ingredients in a large pot without browning them first.

Instant Stock or Bouillon

There are a variety of stock cubes and powders on the shelves of supermarkets and 'health-food' shops. Some of these taste good and others can be

disappointing. When using instant stock powders, work out what concentration suits you. In general 1 level teaspoon of powder (or 1 cube) to 1 cup of boiling water should give a strong enough flavour without being too salty.

Nearly Instant Stock

As an alternative to commercial stock preparations you can make stock almost instantly by dissolving any one of the following in 1 cup of boiling water:

1 tsp Vegemite or Marmite
1 tsp dark (Chinese) soya sauce
1 tsp light (Chinese) soya sauce
1 tsp Kikkoman soya sauce
1–2 tsp miso
1 tsp tomato paste, added to any of the above, improves its flavour.

Experiment with different combinations. My favourite is 1 teaspoon each of light soya sauce and tomato paste per cup of water. It is surprisingly good for something so easy and cheap.

To Serve with Soup

Croutons

Croutons add interesting texture to smooth creamy soups. Spoon or sprinkle them onto individual servings, at the last minute.

2 Tbsp olive or other oil or butter
1 clove garlic
2 thick slices white bread

In a frypan, over a low heat, warm the oil or butter with the sliced garlic. Remove garlic before it browns.

Cut the bread into small cubes, toss in the garlic mixture, then cook on medium heat, turning frequently, until croutons are golden brown, 10–20 minutes.

If preferred, brown under a grill, while watching carefully. Or bake at 150°C for 5–15 minutes or until golden brown. If dried right through, store in airtight containers if not using immediately.

Crostini

Give a Mediterranean touch to your soups. Make these ahead and store in an airtight container to have on hand for guests.

1 loaf French bread
*flavourings ***
¼ cup olive oil

* Parmesan cheese, pesto, tapenade, mixed
mustard, ground cumin, Tabasco sauce

Slice the loaf of bread diagonally into 1cm slices. Mix the flavourings of your choice with the olive oil in a shallow bowl and brush or spread evenly over the sliced bread.

Arrange on a baking tray that has been lightly sprayed or covered with a non-stick or Teflon liner and bake at 150°C for 5–10 minutes until golden brown and crisp.

When cold, store in airtight containers for up to 1 week.

VARIATION: Use slices from any other interestingly shaped or flavoured breads. It is a good way to use up the end of loaves which are a little stale.

Melba Toast

Cut stale bread rolls or French bread into very thin slices, using a sharp serrated knife. Bake at 150°–180°C in one layer on an oven tray until the bread browns very lightly. Cooking time will vary with the type of bread, its thickness and its staleness. Start to check after 3–4 minutes.

When cold store in airtight jars or plastic bags. Refresh for 10 minutes at 150°C before serving if you like.

To Serve with Soup

Garlic Bread

This bread makes a soup meal much more substantial and interesting, especially for family members who are not "wild about soup"! Make it ahead and cook or reheat when needed.

1 loaf French bread (or long bread rolls)
50g butter
2 cloves garlic
2–4 Tbsp finely chopped parsley or other fresh herbs

Cut loaf into diagonal slices 1cm thick, without cutting through the bottom crust, so the loaf (roll) holds together.

Soften but do not melt the butter, then mix in the finely chopped garlic and herbs. Spread the flavoured butter on one side of each cut slice, wrap the loaf in foil, leaving the top exposed, and bake at 200°C for about 10 minutes, or at a lower temperature for longer, until the top crust is crisp and the loaf has heated right through.

Dumplings

Just like grandma used to make! Dumplings absorb some of the soup as they cook, and thicken it slightly, too.

½ cup self-raising flour
pinch of celery salt and garlic salt
1 Tbsp chopped parsley
other herbs to taste, optional
¼ cup milk

Combine ingredients in order given, then stir just enough to dampen flour. Drop mixture in about 12 teaspoon sized amounts into simmering stockbased soup or into stock or water in a pan. Cover pot or pan tightly and simmer for about 10 minutes. Serve immediately.

To microwave dumplings, pour ½ cup of hot water into a 23cm flat-bottomed microwave dish. Drop mixture into water using 2 teaspoons. Cover and cook on High (100% power) for 3 minutes, or until firm. Sprinkle with paprika if desired. Transfer to bowls of piping hot soup.

Cheesy Pastry Croutons

This cheese pastry may be used for many purposes. Children often like to help to cut it into small fancy shapes to float on soup, or into cheese straws to serve with soup.

1 cup flour
1 tsp baking powder
75g cold butter
½ cup (125g) cottage cheese
2 Tbsp grated Parmesan cheese
¼ cup grated tasty cheese
1–2 Tbsp cold water

Put all ingredients except the water into a bowl or food processor. Rub in or process until butter and cheeses are well mixed through the flour.

Gradually add enough water to dampen the dough while stirring or processing in bursts, using the pulse button.

Roll out very thinly. Cut into shapes with small pastry cutters, or into long thin strips. Place carefully on an oven tray covered with a non-stick liner.

Bake at 200°C for 5–10 minutes, or until lightly browned. Watch carefully as they brown very quickly.

Store in an airtight container. Drop in soup just before serving.

Pesto

A spoonful of pesto dropped into tomato soups and some other vegetable soups at serving time adds an "explosion" of flavour and makes the soup much more exciting. Make it during basil's short growing season and keep for later use.

2 cups lightly packed basil leaves
½ cup parsley sprigs
2 cloves garlic
2–4 Tbsp Parmesan cheese
2 Tbsp pinenuts, almonds or walnuts
¼–½ cup olive oil
about ½ tsp salt

Wash the basil to minimise later browning, then drain on a cloth or paper towel. Removing tough stems, put the basil, parsley and peeled garlic cloves in a food processor bowl or blender with the Parmesan cheese and nuts. Process adding up to ¼ cup oil, until finely chopped. Keep adding oil until you have a dark green paste just liquid enough to pour. Add salt to taste.

Store in the refrigerator in a lidded container for up to 2 months or freeze for longer storage.

HINT: Pesto may darken at the top of the jar. Put a layer of oil at the top of each jar, to slow discolouration.

Tomato Salsa

This delicious fat-free sauce makes a great difference to the colour and flavour of soups made from dried lentils and beans.

¼ red onion
1 clove garlic
2 spring onions
2 pickled jalapeno peppers or ¼–½ tsp
*   chili powder*
¼ cup chopped coriander leaves
4 large red ripe tomatoes, blanched or
*   400g can whole tomatoes, drained*
1 Tbsp tomato paste
3 Tbsp wine vinegar
1 tsp dried oreganum
1 tsp salt

Coarsely chop the first 3 ingredients in a food processor. Add peppers or chili powder and coriander, process briefly, then add remaining ingredients and chop just enough to roughly cut the tomatoes. Do not over-process — the mixture should be red flecked with green.

For best flavour, stand for at least an hour before serving. Store, covered, in the refrigerator for up to 2 weeks.

Index

Index

ACKNOWLEDGEMENTS

ALISON'S CHOICE for dried peas, beans, lentils, nuts, pasta and soup mix etc. • **BENNICKS POULTRY FARM**, Buller Rd, Levin, for fresh eggs and table hens • **EMERSON'S BOUTIQUE BREWERY**, Grange St, Dunedin, for beer and ales • **EMPIRE FOODSTUFFS**, for dried herbs and spices • **FERNDALE & MAINLAND** for specialty cheeses • **HARKNESS AND YOUNG LTD**, for Probus utensils • **HORROBIN AND HODGE**, Manakau, for fresh herbs • **J. WATTIE FOODS LTD**, for canned tomatoes and corn etc. • **LAMNEI PLASTICS**, Box 30405, Lower Hutt, for Alison Holst's microwave dishes • **NEW ZEALAND AVOCADO GROWERS ASSOCIATION**, for avocados **PARKVALE MUSHROOMS**, Carterton, for buttons, caps and flat mushrooms • **RON PARKIN**, R.D. 20, Ohau, for fresh asparagus and Genoese Pesto • **S.C. JOHNSON AND SON**, for Chefmate cooking spray • **SOUTHERN OCEAN SEAFOODS**, for fresh and smoked salmon • **TEGEL FOODS LTD**, for poultry • **TUI FOODS LTD**, for Tararua dairy products • **WILLIAM AITKEN AND CO. LTD**, for Lupi olive oil and balsamic vinegar and Azalea grapeseed oil

Knives by Mail Order

For about 20 years I have imported my favourite, very sharp kitchen knives from Switzerland. They keep their edges well, are easy to sharpen, a pleasure to use, and make excellent gifts. These knives are extremely sharp. Please use them with care until you are used to this.

VEGETABLE KNIFE - $8.00 Pointed, straight edged, 85mm blade, in a plastic sheath. Useful for peeling vegetables and cutting small objects.

UTILITY KNIFE - $9.50 Pointed, 103mm blade which slopes back and comes in a plastic sheath. Used for boning meat and general kitchen use.

SERRATED KNIFE - $9.50 Rounded end, 110mm serrated knife in a plastic sheath. This knife should never require sharpening, it will stay sharp for years and is excellent as a steak knife, for slicing bread and fresh baking, slicing tomatoes and fruit.

THREE PIECE SET - $18.00 Serrated knife (as above), 85mm blade vegetable knife with pointed tip, and (right handed) potato peeler.

GIFT BOX KNIFE SET - $38.00 Five knives and a (right-handed) potato peeler. Contains straight bladed vegetable knife, blade 85mm; serrated edged vegetable knife, blade 85mm; small utility knife with a pointed tip blade 85mm; small serrated utility 85mm; larger serrated knife with rounded end 110mm (same as above). ("Straight edge" means that the blade is in line with the handle).

SERRATED CARVING KNIFE - $26.00 Cutting edge 21cm, overall length 33cm. Black, moulded dishwasher-proof handle. Cuts beautifully and never requires sharpening. (Sharpening wears down the serrations.)

STEEL - $20.00 20cm blade, 34cm total length, black, dishwasher-proof handle. Produces excellent results.

KNIFE SHARPENER - $30.00 This sits on a bench, and is held safely, without slipping, with one hand while you draw a CLEAN knife (of any length) through it with your other hand. Easy to use, with two rotating sharpening disks of synthetic ruby. When knife is held vertically, disks are at an ideal angle to sharpen it to a fine point. Do not use with serrated knives. Excellent if you have trouble using a steel efficiently.

For each knife order (of any number of knives) please add $3.50 for packing and postage. All prices inclusive of GST. These prices apply until the end of 1997.

To order send cheque or money order to:

Alison Holst Mail Orders
P.O.Box 17-016
Wellington